BARRIE COUNTRY

Photography and text by
John Bartosik

PHOTOWORKS

Along the Beaten Path

Glacial paths during the ice age were instrumental to the way history unfolded around Barrie Country. After their retreat, lakes, rivers, valley and knoll had formed creating natural waterways and portage routes for the aboriginal people, fur traders, and missionaries, followed by voyageurs in search of the North West Passage. A short walk just east of Barrie's city hall today, was the eastern terminus of the famous Nine Mile Portage, a section of the "Passage de Taronto" linking Lake Ontario and Lake Huron with Lake Ouentaron (Simcoe).

During the War of 1812, a British expeditionary force used this route to relieve Michilimackinac Garrison (near Sault Ste. Marie) besieged by American Forces. At the Willow Creek terminus of the portage, a military encampment and sawmills were established while some thirty bateaux were built and sailed down the Nottawasaga River, to Georgian Bay, and on to Lake Huron to pursue the enemy.

Sir John Franklin, in search of the North West Passage, crossed the Nine Mile Portage with the help of David Soules and his team of oxen from Big Bay Point.

Courtesy of Simcoe County Archives

Barrie's seeds of growth were sewn from a boat landing depot, a Hudson Bay Company storehouse, and a settlement of a few buildings. The site was surveyed, named after Sir Robert Barrie, who at the time was British Commodore of the Great Lakes, and Barrie established roots. The Northern Railway Company brought supplies and pleasure seekers from Toronto; first to Bell Ewart where its steamship was docked, then Allandale in 1853 and later to Barrie in 1865.

The railway transformed the settlement into a provincial town bringing with it prosperity, the advent of lumbering, and new world settlers. Resort vacationers and cottagers from many American Great Lake cities now could access and enjoy the sunny beaches, scenery and fishing at Lake Simcoe, Georgian Bay, and Muskoka.

A group of Dunlop Street merchants. circa 1880

Courtesy of Simcoe County Archives

Barrie then became the gateway to cottage country and the wilderness of the great north. With growth came the great lumbering era and the inevitable exploitation of millions of hectares of seemingly endless forests. Giant stands of hardwoods and virgin pines that stood for untold centuries, with canopies protecting the shaded divine silence underneath, were destined south to supply the growth of cities in Canada and the United States. The cost of building railways was subsidized by granting timber rights. Railroad barons and lumber kings were often one and the same. The rape of the forests came and went with the carrier pigeon.

E.C. Drury, a resident of Simcoe County became Premier of Ontario in 1919 and identified the need for a balance between man and nature. Drury initiated the development of a reforestation policy which led to planting almost a million trees a year on private lands by the Lake Simcoe Forest District by 1971.

Today, Simcoe County's forest lands provide outdoor recreational opportunities, watershed and soil protection and forest products offsetting the cost of operation. In the 1960's, further commercial and residential boom along with tourism brought the construction of Highway 400 connecting Barrie with a continuous route from Toronto to the cottages and towns of Muskoka, and the Trans Canada Highway. Currently, Barrie is a hub for many highway links and is one of the fastest growing cities in Canada.

Barrie's past and future successes are interdependent on it's strategic geographical location. Let us not forget about the ways of the aboriginals; let us perpetuate the abundance of clean water and air, rural countryside scenes, and the natural splendour that still remains—for generations to come.

A view of the west shore of Kempenfelt Bay from the railway line on the south west shore. The steamer Enterprise is shown at Barrie Station Dock. circa 1888

Courtesy of Simcoe County Archives

The stillness of dawn is interrupted by the
roar of the fountain juxtaposed with the
glowing sunrise; creating the illusion of
fire in the sky, at Centennial Beach.

*Fishermen get an early start from
the marina at downtown Barrie.*

*From nearby Moonstone,
Carolyn-Stevens-Sherman
has used more than just a
little paint to refresh this
older shed.*

*Before heading to the
office, golfers leave an
early morning impression
at National Pines Golf
and Country Club.*

*In the spring, and making only
a brief appearance, is one of
the first flora to bloom in the
forest—Ontario's provincial
flower, the trillium.*

Standing as a living monument to
E.C Drury's endevours, is a forest of
white pine near the Midhurst nursery.

Towering over the government
wharf is a seventy foot, steel,
kinetic sculpture called the
Spirit Catcher, by artist
Ron Baird—in the collection
of the MacLaren Art Centre

The south shore community centre has
been redesigned and built from the
original structure of the master
mechanic shop, which is close to the
old Allandale railway station.

Barrie wraps itself around beautiful
Kempenfelt Bay, the deepest part
of Lake Simcoe.

Pioneer days at Simcoe County Museum.

*A re-enactment of the sailing of
bateaux towards Machilimackinac
at historic Glengarry Landing
near Edenvale.*

*Leon Morris from Utopia, and his
team of Belgians Dawn and Lady,
make furrows to plant seed potatoes.*

On weekend mornings, the city hall transforms into a farmers' market of fresh produce, maple syrup, baked goods, crafts, and smiling faces.

Teamwork is exemplified by
members of the Barrie Rowing Club
most early mornings out on the bay.

*A balloon launch is always an awe-
inspiring event to behold that never
seems to dissuade its onlookers.*

A hot air balloon launch at Heritage Park during the Canada Day celebrations.

*During Promenade Days, downtown
Dunlop Street turns into a pedestrian-
only street festival of entertainment
and celebration.*

Sheila Keppler from Bracebridge adds a finishing touch to one of her clowns at Kempenfest; a festival attracting over three hundred artisans spread out along the shoreline of Kempenfelt Bay.

Dressed to the nines for
Canada's Birthday

*Children await the opening ceremonies
for the Highland Games at Burl's Creek
Park. Features include the gathering of
the clans, highland dancers, heavy
events athletes, and the Grand Parade.*

Tania Wattam from Stroud, shows off Amanda at the Barrie Fall Fair and National Horse and Cattle Show.

Barry and Jason Gregg with clydesdale Jonnie, ham it up for the camera during the single draft, workhorse category.

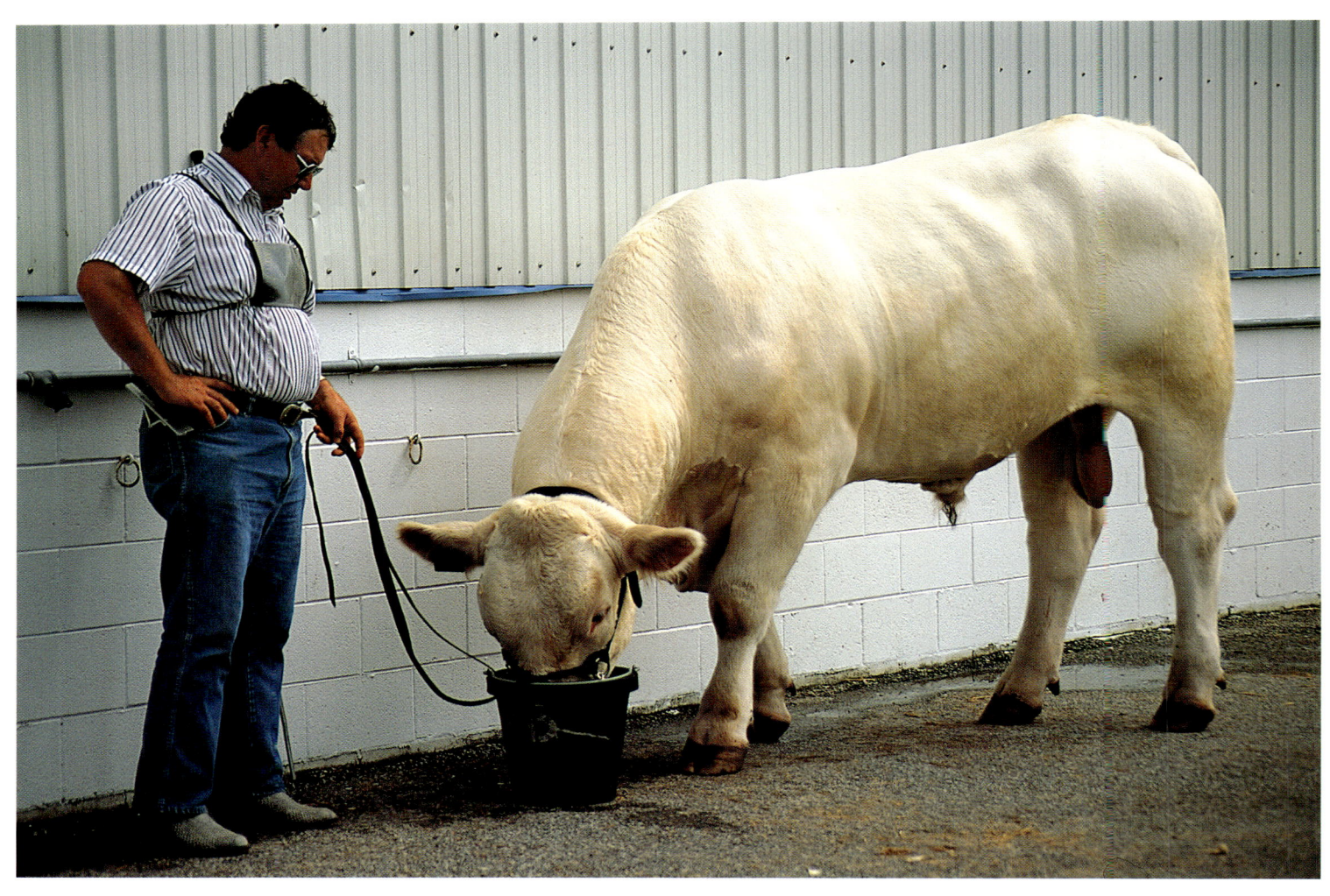

Mr. America, a silver dollar charlois,
gladly laps up a pail of water from
owner Robert Emerson.

Sheena Yarek from Scotland, Ontario,
shows off Wilnorse Red Nugget prior to
the appaloosa breed competition.

Kempenfelt Bay is a jewel,
offering walking and biking trails,
superb beaches, and excellent
conditions for sailing, or
possibly, a sunset dinner cruise
on the Serendipity Princess.

Moses the junkologist sells his
treasures at the Barrie Automotive
Flea Market—cars and parts
as far as the eye can see!

Bob Hillis from Mount Albert, polishes up
his model case tractor at the Beeton
Antique and Steam Show.

During Rendezvous, the Barrie Canoe Club demonstrates the lifestyle of the Voyageurs using bare necessities, including flint.

A young native dancer takes a break at Barrie's Pow Wow, a celebration of native dancing to rhythmic drumming, and singing.

*Harness Racing at Barrie Raceway provides
a popular evening's entertainment.*

*A motocross competition
near Dalston offers many spills
and chills for riders and spectators alike.*

Under the watchful eye of a soldier, a tank transforms into an object of play, at Base Borden, Canada's largest military base near Angus.

Front row centre at the Canadian Forces Base Borden's Airshow.

*Standing alone in a field of
grass, a barn, strong but weary,
reminds us of the early settlers.*

*An aerial view of the
countryside looking south
along Anne Street north.*

*Minet's Point and
a good north-westerly!*

*At night, downtown
Barrie reflects an
irridescent display
of brilliance.*

A seemingly endless country tour leads you down the lane and around the bend, taking you towards yet another magnificent scene.

A sugar shack surrounded by golden coloured maples at Tiffin Conservation Area.

Along Yonge Street (the world's longest), Joseph and Maria Pezzaniti show off their fall harvest, destined to be pumpkin pie for Thanksgiving, or jack-o-lanterns on the neighbour's porch.

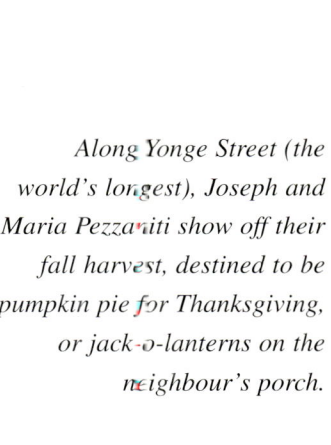

*The "Snowsquall" comes once a
year where man and snowmachine
test their skills.*

A Dogsled Race through the forests
at Tiffin Conservation Area.

A nationals cross-country
ski race at Hardwood Hills.

Snow Valley, Moonstone, and Horseshoe Valley are all within a twenty minute drive from Barrie, offering some of Ontario's finest skiing and snowboarding terrain.

Despite the freezing temperatures,
Winterfest attracts many a brave soul.

*Cousins Andrea and Meghan share a
laugh at the Heights of Horseshoe's
annual Winter Carnival.*

During part of the winter, Kempenfelt Bay
turns into a shanty town of ice huts for
fishermen intent on catching their limit.

Tranquility and solitude are
easily accessible. An abundance
of parkland and trails are scattered
throughout the city and along
its shoreline.

City Hall all dressed up with the
season's snow and colours.

At Fred Grant Square during Winterfest,
an ice sculpture symbolizes Barrie's
many recreational opportunities.

Heavily laden with fresh fallen
snow, pine trees stand defiant to
the previous nights storm along
Horseshoe Valley road.

The cold and snow brings together the community spirit of the Central Ontario Riding Association on an outing through the county forest near Baxter.

Adults and children alike, watch in
fascination as the hot air balloons
descend from the sky to the ice on
Kempenfelt Bay.

Highway 11 just north of Barrie at Gasoline Alley.

To my wife Carol and daughters, Angelaina and Kristin.

Published in Canada by:
John Bartosik

JB PHOTOWORKS
2365 Mapleview Dr.
Stroud, Ontario
L0L 2M0

Art direction, photography, and text by John Bartosik
Graphic design and cover by Jeanette Bartosik

Canadian Cataloguing in Publication Data

Bartosik, John
    Barrie country

ISBN 0-9691873-8-6

    1. Barrie Region (Ont.)—Pictorial works. I. Title.

FC3099.B376B38 1998   971.3'17C98-900402-3
F1059.5.B335B38 1998

Printed and bound in Hong Kong, China
by Book Art Inc., Toronto.